GO FACTS PLANTS
Plants

A & C BLACK • LONDON

Plants

© Blake Publishing Pty Ltd 2002
Additional Material © A & C Black Publishers Ltd 2003

First published 2002 in Australia by Blake Education Pty Ltd

This edition published 2003 in the United Kingdom by
A&C Black Publishers Ltd, 37 Soho Square, London W1D 3QZ
www.acblack.com

ISBN 0-7136-6594-7

A CIP record for this book is available from the British Library.

Written by Paul McEvoy
Science Consultant: Dr Will Edwards, School of Tropical Biology,
James Cook University
Design and layout by The Modern Art Production Group
Photos by Photodisc, Stockbyte, John Foxx, Corbis, Imagin,
Artville and Corel

UK Series Consultant: Julie Garnett

Printed in Hong Kong by Wing King Tong Co Ltd

A & C Black uses paper produced with elemental chlorine-free pulp,
harvested from managed sustainable forests.

What is a Plant?

Plants are living things that use energy from the sun to make their own food.

Plants are living things. All living things can grow, change and **reproduce**. Most living things are either plants or animals.

Plants are the only living things that can make their own food. Leaves are like food factories. Plants take in sunlight, air and water and change them into food. Since plants make food in their leaves, they are the basis for all other life on Earth.

Plants can live in the sea and on the land. They come in all shapes and sizes, from tiny water plants to huge forest trees. Plants grow wherever there is light and water.

Venus flytrap

4

Most plants have flowers.

Waterlilies grow in ponds and lakes.

Plants can live where there is snow.

5

Parts of a Plant

Most plants have roots, stems and leaves.
Many plants also have flowers and fruit.
Each part helps the plant to live and grow.

Roots

Plants have roots under the ground. Roots absorb water and minerals from the soil. Plants need water to live and grow.

Stem

The stem of a plant grows up above the ground.
The stem carries water and minerals up to the leaves.

Leaves

Leaves grow from the stems of a plant. Leaves use the sun's energy to make food for the whole plant.

Flowers

Many plants have flowers. New seeds and fruits grow from flowers.

Fruit

Fruit contain seeds. Animals eat the tasty fruit and the plant's seeds are spread far and wide.

fruit

leaves

flowers

stem

roots

flowers

stem

leaves

roots

7

How Do Plants Grow?

Plants are alive. Like all living things plants grow, change and reproduce.

1 Most plants start life as a seed.

2 From a seed, roots grow down into the soil. The stem grows up towards the light.

3 Leaves take in light energy from the sun. The roots take in water and nutrients. The plant can now make its own food.

4 The adult plant flowers. Inside each flower are eggs called **ovules**. **Pollen** from another flower is carried to an ovule. This is done by the wind or by insects such as bees. The pollen and ovule combine. The petals fall off the flower and seeds grow.

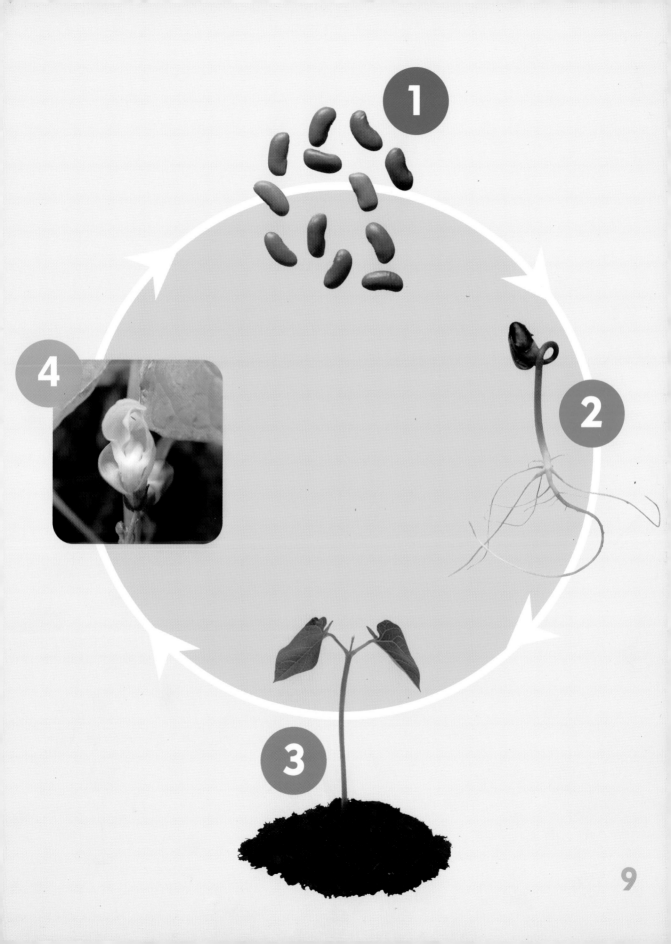

Types of Plants

There are many different types of plants. The land and oceans are full of plant life.

Flowering plants

Flowering plants are the largest group of plants. Most plants have flowers that attract birds and insects. Flowers also attract people.

Towering trees

Trees are the giants of the plant kingdom. Trees provide food, shade and shelter for many living things.

11

Trees, vegetables and seaweed are all plants.

Oceans of life

Some plants live in the ocean. Seaweed, seagrass and **plankton** are types of sea plants. They are the beginning of the ocean's food chain. Fish feed on tiny plankton and other sea plants. Larger sea creatures feed on fish.

kelp

Seaweed can grow in thick clumps.

Dolphins feed on fish.

Plants are food for life

Life on Earth depends on plants. People and many animals need plants to eat. Vegetables, fruits and grains are all important foods for people. About half of the people in the world eat rice every day.

Blackberries are a type of fruit.

Wheat is a grain used to make flour for bread.

Broccoli is a vegetable.

13

Plants for Life

People and animals need oxygen to live. Green plants make the oxygen in the air that we breathe.

How do plants make oxygen?

Plants take in **carbon dioxide**. It enters through small holes on the undersides of their leaves.

Plants absorb sunlight into their leaves. The green substance in leaves is called **chlorophyll**. Chlorophyll traps the energy from the sun.

The leaves use carbon dioxide, sunlight and water to make food and **oxygen**. This process is called **photosynthesis**.

Plants release oxygen from their leaves into the air. Without the oxygen made by plants, animals could not live on Earth.

Energy from sunlight enters.

Carbon dioxide enters from air.

Oxygen is released.

Water comes up from roots.

15

Do Plants Breathe?

Plants breathe through small holes in their leaves. These holes are usually on the back of each leaf.

You can see this happen.

What you need:
- large, fresh leaves
- shallow tray
- magnifying glass
- water and sunshine

What to do:

1 Pick some large green leaves.

2 Pour some water into the tray.
Place the leaves upside down in the tray.

3 Place the tray in a sunny spot and wait for 15 minutes.

4 Look closely at the leaves.
What can you see?

Bubbles come out of each leaf. Each
bubble contains oxygen.

Deserts and Oceans

Plants grow all over the world. Most plants need lots of fresh water but some live where there is very little water — in the desert. Other plants grow where there is only salt water — in the ocean.

Deserts

Water is in short supply in the desert. Sometimes it does not rain for months or even years. When it does rain, the plants flower and make seeds quickly.

Plants that live in the desert need to protect themselves from thirsty animals. Cactus plants grow sharp spines that protect their fat, water-filled stems.

Oceans

The oceans are full of plant life. Water plants, like all plants, give off oxygen. Huge forests of kelp help to keep our air fresh and clean. Half of the oxygen on Earth comes from water plants.

Seaweeds and many other types of **algae** live in salt water. Many sea animals eat these ocean plants.

19

Useful Plants

Plants provide many of the things that people need.

Plants provide us with food. People around the world eat rice, wheat and other grains every day. We also eat fruits and vegetables.

Many oils come from plants. Sunflowers, olives and rapeseed are all grown to make cooking oil.

Trees provide wood and wood products such as paper and cardboard. Wood is used for houses, buildings and furniture. Bamboo and cane are also used to make furniture and baskets.

sugar cane

People grow cotton to make cloth for clothing, sheets and canvas sails. Plants are used to make ropes and nets.

Some medicines are made from plants.

Trees provide wood for house frames.

Wheat is used to make flour for cooking.

Sunflower seeds are mainly grown for their oil.

21

How We Use Plants

Food

Shelter and furniture

Cloth

Other things

WELCOME

Glossary

algae	water plants, such as seaweed and some types of plankton
carbon dioxide	a gas that plants take in
chlorophyll	the part of plants that make them green
ovule	a tiny egg inside a flower
oxygen	a gas in the air that humans breathe to live
photosynthesis	the way plants use energy from the sun to make their own food
plankton	tiny animals and plants that float in the water
pollen	the powder produced by a flower
reproduce	to make new living things

Index